YOUR HIDDEN FEELINGS

Hummu saydee

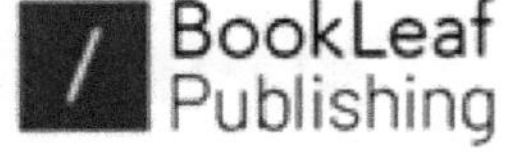

Presentation by *BookLeaf Publishing*

Web: www.bookleafpub.com

E-mail: info@bookleafpub.com

ISBN: 9789357210805

First edition 2022

ACKNOWLEDGEMENT

This would not be possible without a sister who believed in me when I didn't, Aicha." Aicha, thank you for always seeing in me the things I can not see in myself. Thank you for the motivation and the love" and a friend I could call on at any time, Jonathan." Jonathan thank you you for being the listening ears and the super hero who is always to my recus and thank you for also believing in me."

PREFACE

Our unique selves do not look like anyone else.
Our unique selves have our own straight.
Our unique selves have our weaknesses.

What's being nice?

What's being nice

As a child, you find yourself surrounded by
many people you call friends.

You feel loved

You feel liked

You feel belonged

And they all say you are so nice.

As a teenager being in high school and having
the same attention of

being loved

Being liked

And belonging

And they all say you are so nice.

But as you get older and start to grow, you notice a change in you, and you start asking questions like

Why do I feel exhausted when I am around my friends?

Why do they do things to me they don't do to anyone else.

Why do I feel used and abused by people I consider friends?

Why you ask, they say, because you are nice.

So what's wrong with being nice.

Why will people not appreciate a nice person?

Why am I alone crying because I was nice?

Being a nice person may feel good, but it hurts.

It hurts because you give without expectations.

But when you are down, no one offers the same hand you gave out.

It hurts because when you love, you love blindly.

But when you need love, there is no one to give it to you because you made them used to receiving love from you and not giving it back.

It hurts because you show empathy.

But when it comes to you, no one considers your feelings.

You are in the corner crying because

you are exhausted,

You are anxious

It would help if you had a break.

You need to be understood.

You want to be respected and loved and treated like you treat others.

You ask why me?

Where did I go wrong?

What do I need to do?

Just remember

You are beautiful not just because of your looks but your heart.

You have a heart of gold, and the right people will cherish your heart.

Don't change who you are because of the pain you feel. You are needed to remind people to be better.

Learn to love yourself and set some boundaries.
Because being nice is beautiful and precious,
however, not everyone deserves your niceness.

EXPECTATIONS!!

Expectations bring pain. Expectations get us
angry. Expectations get us upset and sad.
Expectations make us want to change who we
are—expectation, Expectation, Expectation.
 Why does it come with all this?
Why, we ask?
We say I'm doing it from my heart.
We say you don't have to pay back.
We say it's okay, don't worry about it.
We say it makes me feel good when I give.
But then why does it hurt when we feel
unappreciated or do not get the same support we
give. Why are we taken for granted, and our
kindness been abused.
We are doing it from the kindness of our heart,
we say, but why are we upset.
The expectation is hiding in the corner of our
minds and waiting.
So are we really kind?
So are we just given without expectation?
Is it really okay?
Let's ask ourselves and be honest with ourselves.
What do we really expect when we give.

TIME

We find ourselves running every day chasing time, and we never seem to catch up to it despite our attempts. At times we look back and hope this is just a dream. We will wake up and be a child again with a clear vision of how to use our time wisely.

 A Question? would you still make the same mistake, or would I take a different approach towards time and decision?

Maybe we should stop hopping; we would have a second chance and put on a watch and make every minute count by planning our life and setting the alarm for every project from when it starts to when it's finished.

We would have to find a way to gain the best from the time we have because every second that passes reminds us that time does not wait for no man.

OUR UNIQUE SELVES.

Our unique selves do not look like anyone else.
Our unique selves have our own straight.
Our unique selves have our weaknesses.
Our unique selves love differently.
Our unique selves do not look like anyone else.
Our unique selves do not have the same straight
as A, B, or Z.
Our unique selves are beautifully unique. Our
unique selves stand out; it adds a special spice to
the world. Our unique selves bring something to
the table that nobody gets. Our unique selves
may feel different but remember your
uniqueness is much needed. Because without
that unique spice, the soup will defiantly not
taste the same.

A Woman.

A woman was not formed but made. God had to be an architect to make a woman.
A woman is beautiful.
A woman can not be defined by just her look or appearance.
A woman is her culture and her clan.
A woman is the backbone of her clan
A woman has a lot of fights in her.
A woman stands on her own two feet when everything seems to crumble.
A woman picks up the crumbled pieces around her, studies them, and turns them into gold.
A woman is not just another creature; instead, she is a masterpiece.

Change

Change comes with growth.
Change can be beautiful; at the same time, it can be painful.
Change does not come to a person who does not crave change because it takes a lot of hard work and determination.
When change is wanted or craved for, your surroundings would need to change; some friends would have to be distant and have a clear vision of what is required.
At times giving up may seem easy, and not understanding the main reason for a change will sabotage your goal for change.
Change is not easy; however, remember your why and find ways to enjoy the process because sometimes a good change is what you need.

Our Quirky Self.

Our quirky self is our secret door to our happy place.
Our quirky self lights up the room with our quirkiness.
Our quirky self does not behave like anyone else in the group.
Our quirky selves laugh out loud because we are free and happy in our skin.
Our quirky self is not worried about what others think about us.
Our quirky self loves being quirky.

Holding-on

Holding-on can be one of the best feelings
Holding on is comfortable.
Holding on is the safety blanket.
however,
Letting go opens an exciting opportunity.
Letting go welcome new blessings
Letting go allows you to grow.
Holding-on can be necessary at some point in
life; however, letting go can be as beautiful, and
it provides the wings to fly and see life and the
world from a different perspective.

The uncertain feeling

We do not know tomorrow; however, the uncertain pain of not knowing lingers around. The uncertain feelings of not knowing if tomorrow will be better than today are the beauty of life.
The uncertain feelings of not knowing if you are making the right choice or not are the beauty of life.
The uncertain feelings of not knowing if your child will be okay is a pain we must endure.
The uncertain feelings of not knowing if your next husband will be better than the last one is a feeling you will have to hold on to.
The uncertain feelings of not knowing if tomorrow will be better than today are the beauty of life because what fun will it be learning about the future before it happens? Life will be boring.
The uncertain feeling of not knowing what tomorrow brings is a surprise, like the feeling of unwrapping a present; we are always anxious to know what the gift is, but just receiving a present is beautiful.

The Crown.

The Crown is not just a headgear that is to be
warned.
The Crown represents power and honor.
The Crown is not to be given to you.
The Crown is you.
The Crown is how you carry yourself.
The Crown is how you talk, walk and interact
with others.
The Crown is you, so make sure you own your
Crown.
Put on your Crown with pride because the
Crown is you.
The Crown is the icing on top of the cake of a
beautiful masterpiece.

Folded Hands

Folded hands make us feel safe.
Folded hands are self-soothing
like a newborn, their palms are folded and
closed
because letting go of our comfort and safe zone
to an unexpected new world may feel scary.
With folded hands, we are being protective; why
don't we let go and allow new things.

MOTHERHOOD

Where do I start? Where do I begin?
It began from the moment I realized I was
pregnant.
The feeling of carrying another life inside me
failed me with fear, love, joy, and peace.
The feeling of being responsible for another life
weighed. Upon like a clock of steel dripped in
steel laying across my shoulders.
 As my child grows, my role grows as a mother,
a teacher, a mentor, and a leader.
This journey never ends. I know one day my
child will have a child, and as I write this, I
begin to smile, and it is now I realize my journey
ends it starts again.

Your Path

Your path may seem dusty
Your path may seem confusing
Your path may seem rocky
Your path may seem intimidating
However
your path is the only path to your success and
your goals.
Your path can be dusted down neatly
Your path can be cleared
Your path can be smooth out
Your path can be an influence
Embrace your path
Learn from the obstacles on your path

Use those obstacles as a stepping stool
Do not give up on your path
Your path is your way through life and yours
alone. Work on it, and you will find your way
through.

GRATITUDE

Gratitude is the key
Gratitude opens doors you do not know excess
Gratitude allows growth
Gratitude opens your eyes to the things you
never knew you had
Gratitude is a healer because it clams your heart
Gratitude is the key, use that key, and you will
be surprised by the blessing you will be walking
in.

EDUCATION

They say education is the key to success.
Is it really?
Some people never went to school, but they still
made it. But how we ask.
If education is the key to success, how did they
make it despite the lack of education?
Remember, education comes in many forms.
At times education comes through a traditional
school.
At times education comes through life
experience.
At times education comes through mistakes.
At times education comes through success.
At times education comes from a five-year-old
who sees life from a different perspective.
Yes, education is the key to success.
Pay attention and educate yourself the way it
comes to you because education is the ladder
you need to succeed.

Those Days

Those days you do not feel like getting up.
Those days when you have your curtains up and
your room still feels like it's midnight.
Those days when all you want is to lay in bed,
rub your bare feet back and forth in your sheet,
and fluff your pillow till it fits your head
perfectly.
Those days are the best.
Those days are rest days.
Those days are self-care days.
Those days allow you to take care of yourself to
take off the people you love.

Your Secret

We all have secrets in our hearts and our minds.
Those precious private things that we will never
shear with anyone, not even our best friends, but
we share them in our diary and pray no one sees
them.
Imagine for just a moment the world knew our
secrets. How would we feel?
What would we say?
I pray that this never happens.
 This reminds us why secrets are secrets and
kept close to the heart and shared with no one
forever and ever.

The Finale

One day it will be our last day, and we will think
of all the things we've done and things we wish
we had done.
Did we tell the right people that we love them?
Did we tell them how special they are
Did we visit the places we wanted to go and do
the things we wanted to do?
We often hear life is too short, but there is
enough time to travel to exotic places, make new
friends fall in love again, and find our happily
ever after.
If we lived a whole life, we would be happy with
who we were, where we went, what we did, and
who we loved.
Hopefully, there will be a smile on our faces, joy
in our hearts, and peace in our souls as we enter
into the hereafter.